Keeping Your Business Organized: Time Management & Workflow

Young Adult Library of Small Business and Finance

Building a Business in the Virtual World

Business & Ethics

Business & the Government: Law and Taxes

Business Funding & Finances

Keeping Your Business Organized:
Time Management & Workflow

Managing Employees

Marketing Your Business

Starting a Business: Creating a Plan

Understanding Business Math & Budgets

What Does It Mean to Be an Entrepreneur?

Young Adult Library of Small Business and Finance

Keeping Your Business Organized: Time Management & Workflow

James Fischer

Mason Crest

Mason Crest
450 Parkway Drive, Suite D
Broomall, PA 19008
www.masoncrest.com

Printed in the United States of America.

First printing
9 8 7 6 5 4 3 2 1

Series ISBN: 978-1-4222-2912-5
Hardcover ISBN: 978-1-4222-2917-0
Paperback ISBN: 978-1-4222-2982-8
ebook ISBN: 978-1-4222-8907-5

The Library of Congress has cataloged the
hardcopy format(s) as follows:

Library of Congress Cataloging-in-Publication Data

Fischer, James, 1988-
  Keeping your business organized : time management & workflow / James Fischer.
      pages cm. – (Young adult library of small business and finance)
  Audience: Grade 7 to 8.
  ISBN 978-1-4222-2917-0 (hardcover) – ISBN 978-1-4222-2912-5 (series) – ISBN 978-1-4222-8907-5 (ebook) – ISBN 978-1-4222-2982-8 (paperback)
  1. Time management–Juvenile literature. 2. Workflow–Management–Juvenile literature 3. Small business–Management–Juvenile literature. I. Title.
  HD69.T54F57 2014
  658.4'093–dc23
                                    2013015650

Produced by Vestal Creative Services.
www.vestalcreative.com

CONTENTS

INTRODUCTION

Brigitte Madrian, PhD

Small businesses serve a dual role in our economy. They are the bedrock of community life in the United States, providing goods and services that we rely on day in and day out. Restaurants, dry cleaners, car repair shops, plumbers, painters, landscapers, hair salons, dance studios, and veterinary clinics are only a few of the many different types of local small business that are part of our daily lives. Small businesses are also important contributors to the engines of economic growth and innovation. Many of the successful companies that we admire today started as small businesses run out of bedrooms and garages, including Microsoft, Apple, Dell, and Facebook, to name only a few. Moreover, the founders of these companies were all very young when they started their firms. Great business ideas can come from people of any age. If you have a great idea, perhaps you would like to start your own small business. If so, you may be wondering: What does it take to start a business? And how can I make my business succeed?

A successful small business rests first and foremost on a great idea—a product or service that other people or businesses want and are willing to pay for. But a good idea is not enough. Successful businesses start with a plan. A business plan defines what the business will do, who its customers will be, where the firm will be located, how the firm will market the company's product, who the firm will hire, how the business will be financed, and what, if any, are the firm's plans for future growth. If a firm needs a loan from a bank in order to start up, the bank will mostly likely want to see a written business plan. Writing a business plan helps an entrepreneur think

Introduction

through all the possible road blocks that could keep a business from succeeding and can help convince a bank to make a loan to the firm.

Once a firm has the funding in place to open shop, the next challenge is to connect with the firm's potential customers. How will potential customers know that the company exists? And how will the firm convince these customers to purchase the company's product? In addition to finding customers, most successful businesses, even small ones, must also find employees. What types of employees should a firm hire? And how much should they be paid? How do you motivate employees to do their jobs well? And what do you do if employees don't get along? Managing employees is an important skill in running almost any successful small business.

Finally, firms must also understand the rules and regulations that govern how they operate their business. Some rules, like paying taxes, apply to all businesses. Other rules apply to only certain types of firms. Does the firm need a license to operate? Are there restrictions on where the firm can locate or when it can be open? What other regulations must the firm comply with?

Starting up a small business is a lot of work. But despite the hard work, most small business owners find their jobs

Keeping Your Business Organized

rewarding. While many small business owners are happy to have their business stay small, some go on to grow their firms into more than they ever imagined, big companies that service customers throughout the world.

What will your small business do?

Brigitte Madrian, PhD
Aetna Professor of Public Policy and Corporate Management
Harvard Kennedy School

ONE

The Connection Between Time and Money

You only have so many hours every day. Sometimes it may seem like you and everyone you know could use a few extra hours in every day. Between school, sports or music, friends, and homework, it's hard to find time to do everything.

On top of that, some young people are interested in running their own businesses. Starting a business and keeping it going takes a lot of time. But plenty of young people have managed it, and so can you. You just need to know how to plan your time and stay organized so you can make it all happen.

Time management involves making the best use of your time, especially if the best use of your time is a task you don't enjoy!

Time Management

The way you keep yourself organized and finish everything you need to do is called time management. Time management includes specific skills and tools like schedules or methods to avoid *procrastination*.

Some people seem to be born knowing how to manage their time pretty well. They seem to be able to do it all—school, friends,

Keeping Your Business Organized

clubs, and maybe even a business. Other people can't seem to get themselves organized. They get up late, forget when homework is due, and don't remember what time to meet friends. Even if you think you're already on top of it all, you can still learn plenty of ways to get even better at time management. And if you think you're hopeless at organizing your life, let alone a business, you can learn ways to manage your time better. Time management is a skill you can learn any time during your life.

In fact, you probably have already had some practice with time management. Business isn't the only place where you need time-management skills. School is another place where organizing your time is really important.

At school, you're used to homework, projects, and tests. All those things have due dates. Maybe you use a planner to organize yourself and keep track of when everything is due. You juggle multiple classes, and have to keep all that information straight in your head. If you have a locker, you figure out when to get your books from it so you're not late to class. You wake up every morning in time to catch the bus or walk to school.

After school and on weekends, you manage to fit in homework and anything else you like to do, like music groups, sports, clubs, or maybe even working at a job. You also manage to have some fun and relax. You probably already have more time management skills than you realized!

Time Management in a Business

Starting and running a business means you'll have to really work on your time-management skills. You'll run into some situations you're not used to at school or at home.

STRESSED-OUT YOUNG PEOPLE

If you're selling things you've made instead of a service, you still need to figure time into your price. Say you make jewelry to sell at craft fairs. You want to first be sure you charge enough to cover the cost of your supplies. Your supplies only cost $1 for each piece of jewelry, so at first it seems like you'll be making plenty of money if you charge your customers $3 for each item. But you haven't taken into account your time yet. If it takes you an hour to make each piece of jewelry, and you charge $3, you'll only be making $2 an hour. Your time is probably worth more than that. So you might want to charge $8 for each piece of jewelry or even $13.

You also have a really good *incentive* to practice time management in your business—because the better you manage your time in business, the more money you'll make! Messing up your schedule or mismanaging your time will mean you're not making as much money as you could. Good businesspeople know how to manage their time.

Imagine you're going to start a pet-sitting business. You love animals, and you've grown up with both cats and dogs. You also want to start making some money, and you're not really interested in working for someone else. You figure a pet-sitting business will be a fun way to start earning and learning about business. So when you sit down to start planning your business, you think about how you're going to manage your time. How

many customers will you be able to handle without going crazy? When will you agree to pet sit, and when will you leave yourself time for homework and dance practice? How will you avoid agreeing to pet sit for two customers at the same time?

Time-management questions are important. Make sure you start thinking of answers before you get your business up and running. You wouldn't want to go through all the work of starting your business and then find out you really don't have time for it!

PRICING ITEMS YOU'VE MADE

If you're selling things you've made instead of a service, you still need to figure time into your price. Say you make jewelry to sell at craft fairs. You want to first be sure you charge enough to cover the cost of your supplies. Your supplies only cost $1 for each piece of jewelry, so at first it seems like you'll be making plenty of money if you charge your customers $3 for each item. But you haven't taken into account your time yet. If it takes you an hour to make each piece of jewelry, and you charge $3, you'll only be making $2 an hour. Your time is probably worth more than that. So you might want to charge $8 for each piece of jewelry or even $13.

How Much Is Your Time Worth?

Part of time management and making money is figuring out how much your time is worth. As a business owner, you're looking for

Figuring out how much your time is worth is based on what other people with similar skills generally charge for their time and how much your customers are willing to pay.

Keeping Your Business Organized

customers to buy whatever you're selling. You need to figure out how much to charge them, which is partly based on how much time you've spent on the product or **service** you're going to sell.

You're not sure how much you should charge for pet sitting. You know you shouldn't charge too much, or no one will hire you. You also don't want to charge too little, because you want to start making money, and you're going to be spending a lot of time pet sitting.

A good way to think about how much to charge is to ask yourself how much your time is worth. You will be working hard to make your business successful, and you already have pet-care skills. Your time is worth something to your customers because they are going to pay you for both your time and your skills.

For a better idea of what to charge, you can ask other people what your time is worth to them. Ask **potential** customers what they would pay. Would your customers pay $20 for an hour of your pet sitting? Would they pay $50? Would $5 be too little? Your customers will tell you the minimum and maximum they would pay. They might think an hour of your pet sitting is worth more than $10 but less than $20. Different people will tell you different things, so look for a range they all have in common.

Take a look at how much similar businesses charge in your town or area too. Say you do some research on pet-sitter prices, and see that the average is about $15 an hour. You see a couple people charge up to $25, but their websites say they are vet technicians who know a lot about animal health. Their pet-sitting time is worth more than yours, because they have more specific knowledge about pets. They have already spent a lot of time learning about pets and can do more with their time pet sitting than you can. You really like pets, and you know how to take

MORE BUSINESS IDEAS

Pet sitting is just one business you could start as a young person. There are plenty of others. Here are just a few:

- Lawn care. Mow lawns, shovel snow, rake leaves, and plant gardens.
- Errands: Offer to help people who can't get around or who don't have enough time. You could do their grocery shopping, pick up things from the drug store for them, and take letters to the post office.
- Crafts: Make jewelry, knit scarves, or create pottery to sell at craft shows, at local stores, or online.
- Create an application: If you're technologically savvy, create games or other applications for computers and smartphones.
- Babysitter: Watch other people's children.
- Tutor: Teach people math, English, history, computers, and more, depending on what you're good at.

basic care of them, but you've never worked in a vet's office. You can't charge as much as the vet technicians can make.

However, your time is worth something! You think about charging $5 an hour. You don't think that's enough, though. You're responsible and you've taken care of your own pets for years. You deserve to make more than that, and you think customers will also be willing to pay you more. In the end, you decide on the

Keeping Your Business Organized

average, which is $15. That seems fair for your customers, and it is also fair for you.

That doesn't mean you yourself are only worth $15. It means an hour of your time is worth $15 to a customer. You can use that information to figure out how to manage the rest of your time.

TWO

Making a Schedule

When you run a business, you'll have lots of things to do. Even just starting a business takes a lot of work. You need to get business *licenses*, buy materials, advertise, and more. Then, once you get your business going, you'll have even more to do! With a schedule, you can keep all your work straight. You can also use a schedule to make sure you don't work too much. After all, you don't want to get stressed out and have to end your business because it's not fun anymore.

Write It Down

One of the first steps of time management is to figure out exactly what you do with all your time. You need to know what you do every day before you can plan your time. Take a few minutes to

Managing your time wisely is a big part of setting and reaching any goal.

Keeping Your Business Organized

write down everything you need to do for your business. Be specific and don't leave out anything. You're making a business to-do list.

If you're just starting out, you might want to keep two to-do lists. One list is all the things that have to get done just to start your business. The other list is all the things you need to do once your business starts selling things.

You'll also want to write down how much time you think each task will take. Creating a website, for example, could take ten hours. Posting flyers in people's mailboxes might take two hours. You don't have to know for sure how long each thing will take, but make your best guess. Knowing the difference between tasks that will take twenty hours and tasks that will take half an hour is a good step in the right direction.

GOALS TO WORK TOWARD

A good scheduling strategy is to make sure you know what your goals for your business are. By defining your goals, you can make sure all the tasks on your to-do list are aimed at achieving that goal. Goals also make it easier to prioritize your to-do list. The tasks that directly work toward your goal are a higher priority than tasks that don't. Some common business goals for young people include making money to buy a car or a bike, saving money for college, helping people out by providing a service, learning about business management, and turning a hobby into a business. Make your goals even more specific, like reaching one hundred people with your product, or making $500 in a year. You may not reach your goal right away, because running a business is hard, but you will be making the right choices to try and get there!

Making a Schedule

23

Prioritization

Your list of things to do might be very long. Some of those things are more important to do than others, though. After you've written down all your tasks, now it's time to prioritize them.

Prioritization means you put the most important tasks at the top of your to-do list. The least important tasks go at the bottom. At the top are things that have to be done. If you don't do them, you won't have a business! To sell handmade jewelry, for example, you have to buy materials and make jewelry. You have to repair your lawn mower to make money mowing lawns.

Farther down the list are tasks that will improve your business. Taking classes, redesigning your business's website, and researching new products to make or services to provide are a little less important than the very first things on your to-do list. They are still important to do eventually, because they will help your business grow, but they don't have to be done immediately.

Another way of thinking of prioritization is to ask yourself which tasks make you the most money. The tasks that are more **profitable** go first. The tasks that won't make you as much money go toward the bottom of your to-do list. Don't worry about making exact calculations—you can just make intelligent **estimates**.

You have a few choices of how to go about prioritizing your to-do list. If you wrote out your list, you can cut it up. Each piece you cut out has one task on it. Then you can rearrange your tasks by moving around the bits of paper. You can also label each task with a number or letter. A or 1 goes to the most important task, B or 2 to the second-most important, and so on.

The easiest way to prioritize is on a computer. You can cut and paste tasks wherever they need to go, without much effort. Play around with the order of the tasks—you can always change

it around if you're not happy with the prioritization the first time around.

Tools

Now that you know how you need to spend your time, create a schedule.

Schedules are time plans, which list out what you have to do, and when you have to do it. They make life a lot easier when you're trying to run a business.

You have plenty of options for how to set up your schedule. You could use a planner, if you like physically writing things down and carrying around your schedule with you. Paper planners come in all shapes and sizes. A giant calendar on your wall that contains the most important things you need to do might also be helpful. Whenever you look at it, you'll remember what you need to do.

You can also use electronic planners. Phones, tablets, and computers all have programs you can use to organize your schedule. Programs you can use include Google Calendar, MS Outlook, and Goalpro. If you spend a lot of time doing business on a computer, or if you carry a smartphone everywhere, an electronic planner might be the best choice for you.

No matter what kind of planner you choose, look for one that suits your needs. You should have enough space to write down everything you need to do. You should be able to enter your schedule easily and quickly. And you should be able to see both day-to-day schedules and longer-term schedules in the same planner.

HOW WELL DO YOU ORGANIZE YOUR TIME?

Do you know how good you are at time management? Take this quiz by answering yes or no to each question, and you'll have a better understanding of your time-management skills. (This quiz was adapted from Mind Tools, a website dedicated to helping people get better at time management.)

- Are the tasks you work on during the day the ones with the highest priority?
- Do you usually finish your work on time?
- Do you set aside time for planning and scheduling?
- Do you know how much time you are spending on various tasks?
- Do you set goals to decide what tasks and activities you should work on?
- Do you leave time in your schedule to deal with "the unexpected"?
- Do you know whether the tasks you are working on are high, medium, or low value?
- Are you able to focus on your tasks rather than get sidetracked by distractions?
- Before you take on a task, do you check that the results will be worth the time put in?

The more yes answers you have, the better you are at time management. Everyone can use some improvement though, so don't get worried or frustrated if you have a lot of no answers. Practice makes perfect!

Keeping Your Business Organized

Making a Schedule

Once you have a planner of some sort, you're ready to start scheduling. Making a schedule can seem like a huge task, but with a little practice, it will become second nature.

First, figure out when you want to work. For your pet-sitting business, you decide you can work Saturdays and after school on Mondays and Fridays. You want to leave yourself time to work on homework, and you have dance practice on Wednesdays. You can also work during school vacations, especially the summer.

Now you need to take a look at your priority list. What are the most important things you need to do to set up your business? What about once your business is running? To set up your pet-sitting business, you have a couple things you know you have to do. You need to make and post advertisements in the newspaper, online, and with flyers around town. You also need to register your business with your town and get a business license. You decide you'll spend your Saturdays working on setting up the business, so you write down your tasks in your schedule. You give yourself three Saturdays of work, and then you hope to have at least one customer. Writing down how much time your work will take is also important. You decide you will work for four hours on each Saturday.

Once you're actually running the business, your priorities for pet sitting are mainly doing the actual pet sitting. You'll be going to people's houses and taking care of their animals while they're away. You don't think you'll be staying over at people's houses very often, just visiting them to feed the animals, clean up after them, give them medicine, and take them for walks. You think you could do two houses in one evening, and three on the weekends. You would spend about an hour at each house, with a few minutes to travel in between the houses. You block out the days you can work on your schedule, and start writing in customers as they contact you. By writing everything down, you can make sure you don't accidentally schedule too many customers on one day.

Your less-important tasks should be scheduled in next. When setting up your business, you have a few things you want to do that aren't as important as your first priorities. You want to do some research on pet care, for instance, so you can be more knowledgeable once you get customers. You decide you'll spend an hour or two researching on Saturdays, once you finish your priorities for the day. You write that in your schedule too.

And later on, you know you'll have to be doing a lot of things to run your business, even though they're not quite as important as actually pet sitting. You want to keep advertising to get new customers all the time. You want to take a class on pet care. You want to build a website. Doing all of those things seems over-whelming! Luckily, with a schedule, you can fit it all in. You decide to fit in your second priorities whenever you have an opening in your pet-sitting schedule. If there's a weekday you only have one customer, for example, you can add some advertising work. If there's a whole weekend day without any customers, you'll put website work into your schedule. Chances are you won't have customers every single night you have scheduled to work.

You may also want to add some time to deal with business problems that come up unexpectedly. A customer might call you at the last minute to pet sit her cat, for example. Or you'll be asked to pet sit a lizard, and you don't really know much about taking care of lizards, so you'll have to do a little research in a short time. You won't always find it possible to schedule in un-expected things ahead of time—but if you know the unexpected could happen sometime in the future, you'll be less stressed out when it does happen. Be **flexible**, but don't be afraid to say no

Keeping Your Business Organized

either. If a customer wants you to pet sit her cat tonight, and you have dance practice, say no.

Now take a look at your schedule. Do you think you can manage what you've set out to do? Businesses take time, but they shouldn't take *all* your time. You should have plenty of time left to go to school, do homework, go to clubs or sports, and just relax. If you think your schedule looks too full, go over it again and make some changes. You may decide to cut out a day of work, or spend less time on your business each day. You can always make changes later, too. Try your business schedule out for a week or two and see if it makes sense for your life.

Finally, you have to schedule in time to schedule! Your planner won't be much use if you never get around to putting anything in it. Make it a point to update your schedule every day, or at least every week. On Mondays, for example, remember to update your schedule. You can even write it in your planner, so whenever you look at Monday, you'll know you need to plan out the week ahead.

A Busy Businessman

Tyler Dikman is a busy man. Now in his late twenties, Tyler got his start in business when he was just five, running a lemonade stand in his driveway. Later on, he had a business as an entertainer at kids' birthday parties; he also babysat and worked for a big company for a summer.

By the time he was fifteen, Tyler had started a company called Cooltronics, a website that sells and sets up computers for customers. During his teen years, he was the founder, president and *CEO* of Cooltronics. His business, even when he was a teenager, had several employees and hired *contractors*.

Tyler Dikman's business sense and time management skills led him to meet not only *Mad Money's* Jim Cramer but two other business giants: Bill Gates and Michael Dell.

"I live, sleep, and walk business twenty-four hours a day," Tyler told an interviewer. "It started as a hobby and fun thing that turned into a whole lot more."

His businesses weren't the only thing keeping Tyler busy. He also volunteered at his church, went to school, and played around on computers in his spare time.

Tyler is a skilled time manager. He learned early on how to organize his time so he could fit everything in. Calling customers, advertising, running a website, managing employees, and more all had to happen every day. Most people would be overwhelmed by all the stuff Tyler had to do. However, he made it happen with great time-management skills. His hard work and organization paid off too—by the time he was seventeen, his company had made more than a million dollars. He went on to found and run more businesses, including Redux, a ***social networking*** website.

Keeping Your Business Organized

Tyler says, "Long hours are all part of the necessary process, but you only live once, and I know that I'll only be successful if I seize the opportunities presented to me." Such a busy schedule isn't for everyone. Most people need some time to relax. But for extremely dedicated business people like Tyler who want to see their companies succeed, a busy (but organized) schedule keeps them going.

THREE

Avoiding Distractions

Television, friends, computer games, movies, and more—you'll find there are a lot of distractions from your business. Good time management lets you get work done when you need to. Then you'll have plenty of time to relax, hang out with friends, and watch TV after you're done.

Unfortunately, it's not that easy. Avoiding distractions can be one of the hardest parts of running a business. Learning how to stay on task and stay away from distractions goes a long way toward making your business a success!

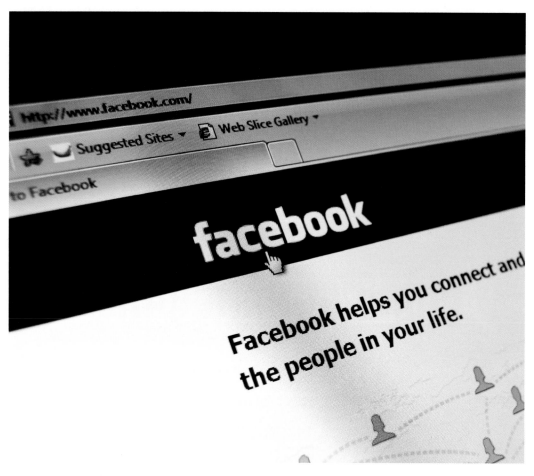

Social networking websites like Facebook can be a very useful tool for many businesses—but they can also be a big distraction!

Potential Distractions

You can probably already list a bunch of distractions. Even if you don't already have a business, you may get distracted in school and while doing your homework.

The computer is the source of a lot of potential distractions. At the same time, chances are good you'll do a lot of the work

Keeping Your Business Organized

for your business on the computer. Computers definitely make it easier to make to-do lists, advertise, and research a **business plan**. The problem is—you can also easily click to the next screen and watch a TV show. Distractions like Facebook, games, articles, blogs, and more are just a click away.

Friends and family can also be distractions. You could be working away during your scheduled business block of time when your friend starts to chat with you online. Then another friend calls you, and you talk with him for an hour instead of telling him you'll call back when you're done working. Your little sister might come into your room and start bothering you, making it hard for you to concentrate.

Imagine you're working on creating your new website so more people can find your business online, and can figure out how to contact you. You're really excited about the website, but it's proving to be harder than you thought it would be. You've scheduled yourself a week to finish the website—one hour each evening. The first day you spent the whole hour working on the website, but the second day you got distracted. Your friend started chatting with you online, and you focused on talking to her instead of creating your website. Pretty soon, your hour was up, and you had to start doing homework.

The next day, you sit down at the computer again. But this time, you just can't stop thinking about the new episode of your favorite TV show that just came out online. You end up watching it instead, and your hour is up again.

Now you've wasted two whole evenings of website work! You only allowed yourself one week to finish it, because next week you have a lot of pet sitting to do. How will you stay on track for the rest of the week and get your website done?

PROCRASTINATION

We all avoid doing things from time to time by telling ourselves we'll do them later. Avoiding important tasks is called procrastination. Everyone procrastinates at least once in a while, but some people procrastinate all the time. Procrastination can really get in the way of running a successful business, so you want to get your procrastination under control.

Avoiding calling an important customer to let her know her order will be late by playing a video game instead is a good example of procrastination. Talking to your customer might not be a pleasant experience, but you have to do it. As you can guess, the longer you wait to call the customer, the angrier she may get. If you tell her right away, she'll know not to expect her order on time.

You have several ways to beat procrastination and stay on top of your business. Prioritized schedules work. Do your most important tasks first, and don't move on until they're done. Another helpful strategy is to break your tasks down into smaller chunks. Sometimes we procrastinate because we're overwhelmed by what we have to do. Instead of telling yourself you have to create an entire website, for example, tell yourself you only need to design the homepage first. Then you can work on the other pages another time.

Solving the Distraction Problem

You know you want to make your business work, but all these distractions make it hard to get down to it! To really dedicate yourself to your business, you'll have to get rid of distractions.

Keeping Your Business Organized

One thing you may want to do is keep a list of all the distractions you face during a week. Write down everything that distracts you from doing the work you should be doing. Also write down the time you get distracted, and how long you're distracted. Be honest. Your distraction journal will help you from here on out, but it will only help you if you're truthful.

Your distraction journal for pet sitting might look something like this:

Day 1, 6:45 P.M.: Mom came into room and asked about lunch tomorrow, 3 minutes.
Day 2, 8:05 P.M.: Started chatting with Maria online, 50 minutes.
Day 3, 8:10 P.M.: Watched TV show, 50 minutes.

Now you can compare your distractions to each other. You see that the first day you started a little earlier. Your mom interrupted you, but you got right back to work. You think maybe you should tell your mom to wait to ask questions until after you're done with your business work.

You also notice that you got distracted when you worked later. Maybe you're more tired at 8:00, so you should always try to start earlier. You also see that the computer is your source of distractions. You decide you're going to plan as much of your website as you can on paper before you start making it on the computer. You'll also turn your chat program off, so your friends can't talk to you.

But sometimes distractions will just happen naturally. You have to know how to deal with the distractions that do arise, and learn how to keep going with your work instead of paying attention to the distraction.

Now that many of us carry around our e-mails wherever we go, this form of communication has gotten very convenient but also very distracting.

Keeping Your Business Organized

E—MAIL DISTRACTION

E-mail might end up being a big part of your business, because it's how you keep in contact with people. But e-mail can also be a huge distraction. You may end up reading a long e-mail from a friend on vacation instead of answering a customer's e-mail. Or you might read and answer a lot of e-mails instead of doing something more important and urgent, like attending a meeting or getting to an event on time where you're selling your product. Keep e-mail from becoming a distraction by scheduling times in your workday you can look at and respond to messages. You could set aside ten minutes every evening you work, for instance. Once those ten minutes are up, you have to move on to different tasks. Answer the most important e-mails and leave the least important ones for later when you have some free time. You can also write "answering e-mails" on your schedule, and fit it in that way.

For example, you can't help getting phone calls. You could shut your phone off during your work hours, but what if you need to use it? You might be expecting a call from your mom. Or what if a customer needs to call you? Instead, learn to screen your calls instead of answering every one (or answering text messages). Only answer calls from your mother or that have to do with your business. Ignore friends or other calls and texts until you have time to answer them. You can let your friends know that you won't answer them while you're working, but you'll call them back a little later.

If someone needs to talk to you right away—your mom, for example—keep the conversations short. Tell the person you're

Taking a break every once in a while keeps you productive and gives you a chance to check your phone, eat some food, and think about something other than work.

Keeping Your Business Organized

working hard on your business and you only have five minutes to talk. Don't be rude. Listen to what they have to say, just let them know you don't have time to talk for an hour.

You should also let yourself have breaks. If you've scheduled yourself to work for five hours on a weekend day, don't expect yourself to work for all five hours straight. People need breaks to stay *productive*. Without breaks, you actually do less work, because you'll get tired and bored. Let yourself take a break and do something a little distracting every couple hours. Keep your breaks short, though, or you'll never go back to work.

FOUR

Organizing Records: Setting Up a System

Maybe you've figured out how to manage your time, and you're learning to manage distractions—but how about your workspace? Organizing your workspace and your records helps your business run more smoothly and **efficiently**. As long as you know where everything is, you can find what you need, when you need it. That will save you time too.

The purpose of organization is to make it easier for you to do business. An organized business will also make you more money. When customers see you're organized, and can retrieve information quickly, they'll be impressed and want to hire you or buy from you. When you're disorganized and can't seem to keep track of orders or remember to call customers, you won't get very far.

Whether your files are real or on a computer, keeping them organized will save you time, money, energy, and frustration.

 **Keeping Your Business Organized**

Don't worry if you're not naturally an organized person. Anyone can learn how to be more organized. All it takes is a little practice and patience.

Office Space

What sort of space do you use for your work? Maybe you've set up a small office in your bedroom. Maybe you work out of a backpack, wherever you can find room. No matter where you work, it's in your best interest to keep your workspace organized.

Only use what you really need. Do you really need two staplers, a glue stick, fifteen pens, and several stacks of Post-it® notes at your desk? Probably not. Stick to what you really need, and keep the rest of your stuff somewhere else.

If you have a workspace in your bedroom, you may be tempted to clutter it with things that aren't related to your business. Try to keep your workspace for work. If you have to use your desk for homework or other things, keep your different papers separated. You don't want to accidentally turn in your business plan to your English teacher instead of your essay!

You may need to keep physical copies of files on hand. You may have signed business licenses, copies of **tax** forms, and letters from customers. Figure out a system that keeps your papers organized. Get a file cabinet or even just a file box, and divide it into colored and labeled folders. Have one folder for licenses, one folder for tax-related files, and one folder for customers. Add as many folders as you need. Label each folder on its tab, and keep all the folders in alphabetical order. When you need to find something, you'll know exactly where to look.

Knowing how to organize your desk means a lot more than just keeping it clean!

Keeping Your Business Organized

DESK ORGANIZATION TIPS

Your desk can easily become the messiest place in your workspace. Here are a few tips to keep it clean and organized, so your work goes smoothly:

- Organize your drawers by priority. Keep the most important things in the top drawer, and the things you use the least in the bottom drawer. It's easier to pull out the top drawer, and more of a hassle to reach down to the bottom.
- Spend five or ten minutes cleaning up at the end of each workday. Even if you only work for an hour during the evening, make sure you organize and clean up before you quit for the night.
- Keep a recycling bin and a garbage can next to your desk. When you need to get rid of something, you can toss it instead of letting it sit on your desk for weeks.
- Have a box or bin where you keep projects you're working on right now. Everything else can be stored somewhere out of sight, like in a filing cabinet. Only keep the things you really need for your business right away on top of your desk.

An Organized Computer and Phone

Your desk and other workspaces aren't the only places you work. You also probably work on your computer and keep records there. Maybe you even run your entire business online. Keeping track of records and business documents is key to running a great business.

Organizing Records 47

Organizing your computer files won't only make it easier to find them but will make you better prepared and more professional.

Keeping Your Business Organized

For your pet-sitting business, for example, you might keep records of all your customers on your computer. You have a file for each customer and his or her pets. The files have important information, like the personality of each pet, the medications it takes, and the care it needs. Your customers trust you to remember their pets' information every time they hire you.

Your computer and your smartphone help you run a good business. The problem is, you keep losing the files on your computer. You never remember where you put them, and you've lost a few. Sometimes you show up at customers' houses without all the knowledge you need, which makes you look unprofessional.

Your solution is to start organizing your files using your own system. You decide you're going to name all your pet-sitting files using the same system. Each file will be named using the family's last name, followed by a dash and the animal's name. Every pet will have its own file. And all those files will be organized into a folder called "Pet Sitting," which is further divided into folders for each year you're in business. When you have the same customers from year to year, you'll copy over their file into the new year. That way, you can keep track of the pets' information, and also see what year customers first started hiring you.

When you started your business, you also **invested** in your own smartphone. You wanted to keep your schedule on it, to keep track of when you needed to take care of pets. You also wanted to be able to look up any pet-care information you needed while you were pet sitting.

One day, you drop your phone and it breaks. Not only do you have to buy a new phone, your schedule and all your contacts are gone! You never wrote them down anywhere else. Now you can't easily call that customer you told you'd update about his pet. You can't tell if that's a customer calling you or your friend. And you don't remember when any of your pet-sitting appointments are!

Organizing Records 49

Backing up your contacts in a Rolodex like this one will prevent you from losing them if anything ever happens to your smart phone or computer.

Keeping Your Business Organized

You end up going through the phone book and calling all the customers you think had hired you for the upcoming weeks. Even so, you miss one appointment. The customer gets angry and refuses to hire you again. Your mistake has cost you a customer, and you vow to keep your schedule and contacts written down as well as on your new phone.

You've learned two very good lessons about electronic organization. Keep your computer files organized so you can find them easily. Organize your files by date, and use the same system for naming all files. And always back up all your records. Keep a copy of your contacts in multiple places, like on your phone and on your computer. Back up other records too, whatever is important for your business. You never know when your computer or phone will crash or break.

You can use an **external hard drive** to back up your files. You can also use online storage services like Dropbox or iCloud. You can save files from all your electronic devices on them quickly and easily. Computers can make organization easy!

FIVE

Creating Good Habits to Keep You Going

Habits are things we do that are automatic. You don't have to think about doing a habit; you just do it. Habits can be hard to start, but they're also hard to break once they're established. You'll find it's worth your effort to create good business habits to keep you going.

Good Habits and Bad Habits

Habits can be either good or bad. A better way of thinking about them is to look at habits as healthy or unhealthy.

Healthy habits keep you healthy and happy. Brushing your teeth is a good example of a healthy habit. When you were little, your parents may have had to tell you to go brush your teeth every morning and night. You never remembered, and you may never have wanted to do it. By now, though, you're used to brushing your teeth. You may not even really think about it anymore—you just do it. Brushing your teeth has become a habit. It feels like it takes very little effort to brush your teeth every day. It's just something you do without even thinking, and it helps keep you healthy.

Unhealthy habits, however, get in the way of your health. You may think unhealthy habits are making you happy, but in the long run, you'll be less happy. Watching too much TV is an example of a bad habit. Whenever you get home from school, you go straight to the TV and end up watching it for a few hours. You would be better spending that time doing your homework or working on your business. You also get in the habit of just sitting and not moving around. Over time, the lack of exercise will cause weight gain and health problems.

Good Business Habits

We can follow good and bad habits in our everyday lives. We can also follow good and bad business habits. Business habits are the things we do automatically when it comes to jobs, work, and companies. The point of good business habits is to make your business work better and your life easier. Good business habits lead to more satisfied customers and more work done.

The first step to having good business habits is knowing what good business habits are. We've already covered a few of them: making and sticking to a schedule, avoiding distractions and staying focused, and keeping your workspace and computer organized.

Being on time is also a good business habit (and a good habit to have in general). Get to meetings on time. Meet customers at

Keeping Your Business Organized

the time you say you're going to meet. Make it to the printer on time before the store closes. Being *punctual* helps your business out a lot.

Friendliness is another good business habit. Some people are naturally friendly, while others have to work on it because they are shy or less open. When you're friendly, you end up with better relationships with your customers and other people who help your business run smoothly. Being friendly means greeting people with a smile, being pleasant on the phone and in e-mail, and keeping your temper under control.

BAD BUSINESS HABITS

Along with good business habits, there are plenty of bad ones. Just about everybody has a bad habit or two, which can get in the way of making your business as successful as it can be. Instead of thinking about breaking these bad habits, you might find it more helpful to think about replacing them with good habits. Take a look at these bad habits, and their better replacements.

Bad Habit	Better Habit
Being late all the time	Getting ready to go ten minutes before you would normally
Making *impulsive* decisions	Creating a pro and con list before making big decisions
Procrastination	Focusing on your work and turning off all distractions

Finishing what you start is also a good business habit. The best businesspeople start a project—like an advertising **campaign** or creating a new product to sell—and then they finish it. The project may take them a long time, but they stick with the work. In the end, they have a better business and more sales because they took responsibility for finishing what they started rather than jumping around from project to project that never gets done.

Making Good Habits Happen

Creating good habits can take some work, but the good news is that anyone can form new habits. You just have to want to create those habits. By focusing on good habits, you can make bad habits disappear. Focus on how much better your business will do if you focus on good habits, and you'll stay **motivated**.

Scientists have found that actions take an average of sixty-six days to become habits (a little more than two months). Some people may need more or fewer days, depending on who they are and what habit they're trying to learn.

You may need to try a few different ways of replacing bad habits or forming good habits. Don't give up, though! You'll figure out the right way, and then you'll be well on your way to a more successful business.

First, create a plan. What are your habit goals? Don't start too big, by tackling all the good business habits you want at once. Start with one habit you think is important to have.

Maybe you really want to arrive on time at each of your pet-sitting customers' homes. You tend to get to each appointment fifteen minutes late. You know you sometimes make your customers worry or even make them mad. You want them to trust you, though, and you don't want to start each job with an angry customer.

Add your new habit to your to-do list. Write the good habit you want on your list every day. You can even write it multiple times in one day. Even when you're not looking at your to-do list, remind yourself whenever you can about your new habit. The more you remind yourself you want to create a new habit, the better your chances of sticking with it.

For each appointment you have, you write down what time you need to leave your house, or wherever you'll be traveling from. You use online maps to figure out how long it takes you to get to your customers' houses. Then you add on ten minutes, just to be sure. Finally, you write down those times for every single appointment in your schedule. You write, "Be on time!" at the top of every to-do list.

Ask other people to remind you of your new habit, too. Tell your family and friends what you're trying to do. Then get them to remind you of your new habit whenever they see you. If they notice you're not following your habit, they can gently remind you and tell you what you need to do.

For example, you tell your parents you're trying to get to your pet-sitting appointments on time. You show them your to-do list and schedule, so they know what time you need to leave your house. Your dad gets really into helping you, and he reminds you whenever he can about your goal. Sometimes you get annoyed when he tells you it's time to get going to your job, but you know he's helping.

Don't get too frustrated if you find yourself slipping every now and then. Creating a habit isn't easy. Just because you make a mistake doesn't mean you've failed. You just need to keep trying. The longer you try, the easier and easier it will become to reach your goal. After a while, you won't need to think about what you should be doing. You'll just do it! Then you've created a habit.

Creating Good Habits

So at first, you'll struggle with leaving on time for your appointments. Something always seems to come up right before you have to leave, or you forget you need to go until it's too late. But you try really hard, and slowly you start leaving on time just about every day. After three months, you find yourself leaving on time automatically. You don't have to write it down on your to-do list anymore, and you don't need your parents' reminders, because you've gotten used to thinking about leaving on time. You do still write down the times you need to leave in your planner, to be extra sure. You've created a good habit—and your customers are happier!

Lizzie's Habits

Lizzie Marie Likness is a young businessperson who knows how valuable good habits are. Lizzie started a healthy food business when she was just six. She started selling baked goods at a farmers' market to make money to pay for horseback riding lessons. Soon, she created a website and started her own company, Lizzie Marie Cuisine.

Lizzie was used to working hard even when she was very little. She says, "Once I started realizing how much people enjoyed my cooking and how much I enjoyed getting up early in the morning and baking and seeing people's faces once they tried my food, that's when I wanted to take it to the next level." Even when she first started out, Lizzie created the habit of getting out of bed early to work on her business. She scheduled each Saturday for baking and selling her food.

Not everyone thought such a young kid had the ability or the habits to run a business. "A lot of people were surprised at how young I was," Lizzie explains, "because they didn't think a

six-year-old could be in the kitchen, baking breads and cookies. Once they got over that, they were pleasantly surprised and said the food was good and healthy."

Interacting with customers taught her how to be friendly. Selling at a farmers' market taught her how to be on time, even early in the morning. Lizzie also learned plenty of other good habits for her business because she has done a lot! She creates videos for her website; she has spoken at American Heart Association events; she teaches elementary school students about healthy eating; and she has filmed online videos for the health website WebMD. She has to keep all that straight by prioritizing her time and scheduling it.

Lizzie doesn't plan on slowing down in the future. She says, "I'm working on a cookbook for kids and adults, because I'm all about having kids come into the kitchen to help their parents cook. I'm talking with some big food names—I can't say who right now—about partnering up and possibly creating a **brand**, having different products, and things like that. I think it would be cool to have a line of cookware, like Rachael Ray does. I definitely have exciting projects coming up that will help Lizzie Marie Cuisine become even bigger."

Her future projects will help her learn even more good habits. Running a business is a learning experience. Young people like Lizzie and Tyler Dikman have learned plenty of good habits from their businesses, like scheduling, responsibility, and organization, but they can learn even more.

As you run your own business, you will also figure out how to manage your time, keep yourself organized, and build good habits. The end result of all your hard work will be a better business—and more satisfaction with a job well done.

Find Out More

ONLINE

Biz Kids
www.bizkids.com

Mind Tools
www.mindtools.com/index.html

PBS Kids: Time Management
www.pbskids.org/itsmylife/school/time

IN BOOKS

Bachel, Beverly K. *What Do You Really Want? How to Set a Goal and Go for It!* Minneapolis, Minn.: Free Spirit Publishing, 2001.

Bochner, Arthur and Rose Bochner. *The New Totally Awesome Business Book for Kids*. New York: Newmarket Press, 2007.

Mariotti, Steven. *The Young Entrepreneur's Guide to Starting and Running a Business*. New York: Times Books, 2000.

Vocabulary

Brand: a type of product made by a particular company.

Business plan: a document that outlines the reasons for setting up a business, and details how the business will be run.

Campaign: an organized course of action with a specific goal.

CEO: Chief Executive Officer; the person in charge of running a company.

Contractors: people hired temporarily to do a job.

Efficiently: quickly and with a minimum of waste.

Estimates: guesses.

External hard drive: a storage device that holds electronic data independently of a personal computer.

Flexible: able to change when the situation calls for it.

Licenses: permissions to do something, often given by the government.

Impulsive: acting without thinking first.

Incentive: something that motives or encourages a person.

Invested: devoted money, time, or effort to something with the expectation of achieving a worthwhile result.

Motivated: to have interest and enthusiasm to do something.

Potential: having the ability to become or develop into something greater.

Procrastination: putting off doing important tasks in order to do less important tasks.

Productive: able to create useful results.

Profitable: money-making.

Punctual: on time.

Service: action performed for someone's benefit.

Social networking: the use of websites and computer applications to communicate with a large group of people.

Tax: money collected by the government to pay for services like roads, schools, and parks.

Index

About the Author and Consultant

James Fischer received his master's in education from the State University of New York, and went on to teach life skills to middle school students with learning disabilities.

Brigitte Madrian is the Aetna Professor of Public Policy and Corporate Management at the Harvard Kennedy School. Before coming to Harvard in 2006, she was on the faculty at the University of Pennsylvania Wharton School (2003–2006), the University of Chicago Graduate School of Business (1995–2003) and the Harvard University Economics Department (1993–1995). She is also a research associate and co-director of the Household Finance working group at the National Bureau of Economic Research. Dr. Madrian received her PhD in economics from the Massachusetts Institute of Technology and studied economics as an undergraduate at Brigham Young University. She is the recipient of the National Academy of Social Insurance Dissertation Prize (first place, 1994) and a two-time recipient of the TIAA-CREF Paul A. Samuelson Award for Scholarly Research on Lifelong Financial Security (2002 and 2011).

Picture Credits